THE INDIAN OCEAN

BY JUNIATA ROGERS

Published by The Child's World®
1980 Lookout Drive • Mankato, MN 56003-1705
800-599-READ • www.childsworld.com

Credits: alpinenature/Shutterstock.com: 6; alybaba/Shutterstock.com: 21;
Creative icon styles: 5 (compass); Drew McArthur/Shutterstock.com: 10; Ethan
Daniels/Shutterstock.com: 13; Hendrik Martens/Shutterstock.com: cover, 1;
Janos Rautonen/Shutterstock.com: 18; Matyas Rehak/Shutterstock.com: 9;
Shandarov Arkadii/Shutterstock.com: 17; VladSV/Shutterstock.com: 15

ISBN HARDCOVER: 9781503825031
ISBN PAPERBACK: 9781622434350
LCCN: 2017960229

Printed in the United States of America
PA02373

TABLE OF CONTENTS

WHERE IN THE WORLD?

Where is the Indian Ocean? Look at the map. Can you find Africa? It is to the ocean's west. Now find Asia. It is to the north. Australia is to the east and south. The Indian Ocean is between them all.

The Indian Ocean mixes with three other oceans: The Pacific, the Atlantic, and the Southern.

The Indian Ocean is the third largest ocean.

The Indian Ocean is named for the country of India. The ocean surrounds India on three sides.

GREAT FOR A DIP

The Indian Ocean is mostly warm. It stays warm all year. This water is warm enough for swimming. But not in the far South. There, it is cold all year.

The Indian Ocean is the warmest ocean on Earth. It stays above 71 F (22 C) all year. The water gets colder near the Southern Ocean.

CHANGING WIND

Monsoons are winds. They change with the seasons. In winter, they bring dry weather. In summer, they bring rain. In some areas of the world, monsoons can bring so much rain, flooding happens.

Monsoons always blow from a colder area to a warmer area.

In India, much of the country's rain for the whole year falls during the summer monsoon season.

Cyclones are stronger over the ocean water. They weaken once they reach land.

TOO MUCH WIND!

Cyclones can come with the rain.

Cyclones are big storms. They bring high winds and floods. They can bring danger, too.

In North America, cyclones are called hurricanes.

CHANGING WATER

A **current** is fast water. It always goes the same way. At least, most currents do. The Indian Ocean has an odd current. It turns around. In summer, it goes west. In winter, it goes east. It is the only current that changes like this.

The Java Trench is the deepest place in the Indian Ocean. It is a little more than 4.5 miles (7 km) deep.

Ships that carry oil
are called tankers.

AN OCEAN FOR OIL

There is oil under the Indian Ocean.

People drill for it. They load it on ships.

The ships take it from **port** to port. This

makes the ocean busy!

The Suez Canal connects the Indian Ocean to the Mediterranean Sea.

A GOOD HOME

The Indian Ocean is a good home.

Many animals live there. Sea turtles call

the Indian Ocean home. So do shrimp,

crabs, and fish. Dugongs are big sea

animals. They live in the Indian Ocean's

warm waters.

Dugongs are relatives of the manatee.

Some people think dugongs inspired the first stories of mermaids.

Hammerhead sharks love to eat stingrays.

Whales and dolphins live in the Indian Ocean. So do many kinds of sharks. Hammerhead, dusky, and great white sharks all feed on the smaller fish.

Elephants sometimes swim in the Indian Ocean. They use their trunks like snorkels.

AN IMPORTANT PLACE

The Indian Ocean is lively. It is always

changing. Many people and animals call

it home. It is an important part of Earth.

The Indian Ocean is getting almost 8 inches (20 cm) wider each year. This is because of the melting ice in Earth's much colder areas.

The Indian Ocean covers 1/5 of the world.

GLOSSARY

current (KUR-rent): A current is a flow of water in a river or ocean. In the ocean, a current always takes the same basic path.

cyclone (SY-klohn): A cyclone is a big and powerful storm that forms in oceans over warm water.

monsoon (mon-SOON): A monsoon is the name for a wind on the Indian Ocean that changes direction by season. The word "monsoon" is also used for the season of rainy weather that comes with the wind, and for the rains themselves.

port (PORT): A port is a town where boats come and go. There, they load and unload goods.

TO FIND OUT MORE

Books

Oachs, Emily Rose. *Indian Ocean*. Minneapolis, MN: Bellwether Media. 2016.

Spilsbury, Louise, and Richard Spilsbury. *Indian Ocean*. Chicago, IL: Heinemann Raintree, 2015.

Wilsdon, Christina. *Ultimate Oceanpedia: The Most Complete Ocean Reference Ever*. Washington, DC: National Geographic Children's Books, 2016.

Woodward, John. *Ocean: A Visual Encyclopedia*. New York, NY: DK Publishing, 2015.

Web Sites

Visit our Web site for links about the Indian Ocean:
childsworld.com/links

Note to Parents, Teachers, and Librarians: We routinely verify our Web links to make sure they are safe and active sites. So encourage your readers to check them out!

INDEX

ABOUT THE AUTHOR

Juniata Rogers grew up in Newport, RI, an island town on the Atlantic Ocean. She has worked as a naturalist, an art model, and a teacher. She's been writing professionally for 25 years, and currently lives near Washington, DC.